Love Letters from Cuckold Creek

poems by

Kristin Kowalski Ferragut

ISBN: 978-93-6354-819-0

First Edition: 2025
Rs. 200/-

Cyberwit.net
HIG 45 Kaushambi Kunj, Kalindipuram
Allahabad - 211011 (U.P.) India
http://www.cyberwit.net
Tel: +(91) 9415091004
E-mail: info@cyberwit.net

Printed at Repro India Limited.

For Quinn and Coley

with infinite love.

For Kathy Stecke

I'm grateful my younger self

had such a great hero.

And I still do.

For Baeley Aubrey Thackston

and all those who love him and

uplift his life every day.

J.J.B

Acknowledgements

Gargoyle Magazine Online #12, February 2025: "Memory's Intrusion" and "Stars Bend Light, Erase Habit of Devotion"

Gargoyle Magazine Online #4, February 2023: "Celebration of Survival," "Seems We Fall in Buddhist Surrender," and "Empathy"

Mid-Atlantic Review, Fall 2024, "Alive on Cuckold Creek I", "Alive on Cuckold Creek II", "Creative Seeing"

Live Encounters American Poets and Writers, January 2022: "Falling"

Maryland Literary Review, 2023 Fall/Winter: "Monody"

Beltway Poetry Quarterly, Fall 2021, "Near to Life"

I am also grateful to Grace Cavalieri, Kelly Catherine Bradley, and Le Hinton for their inspiration, light, and kind words — to have their blurbs on this collection is a dream. I thank all of my poet friends who support and inspire me and my work, including Luther Jett, Alison Palmer, Serena Agusto-Cox, Lucinda Marshall, Mabel Ferragut Smith, Indran Amirthanayagam, Tracey Lenhardt, Sandra Lawson, Kevin Farragher, and Jay Hall Carpenter. And I shout out to my poetic musician friends who help fuel my creativity and courage — Lisa Marsh, Laura Outerbridge Evans, Beth Riley, Patty Raine, Eddie Kowalski, Greg Marsh, Rich Morey, Jeff Jones, Wayne Cobb, Carolyn Rooney, Michael Occhionero, and Craig Allison. Thanks also to my Mom and all my family, and Tammie Snyder and Jen Best who defy category.

“If you search everywhere, yet cannot find what you are seeking, it is because what you seek is already in your possession.”

-- Lao Tzu

Contents

*

Untangle

As a girl, my one skill was taking apart knots.
For hours fingertips loosened, puzzled, tightened,

again and again. I might've described unknotting
like I later spoke of walks, "Anywhere
is walking distance if you have the time."

That's to say my one skill
is perseverance.

I might watch light
arc through hours, holding mortality, dangle
a dream on the exhale
of the clock's second hand.

I missed the magic of space, less
the window-view of sunset on water and more
how you stopped posturing and noticed

in silence. Having happened once meant
it might again.

Wishes hung on possibility drip
dust and effort until I become
an unraveled drape, glass knick-knack,
a haunted house. Safe in being

covered, tangled,
forgotten. Loosen and puzzle, tighten, start again.

Monody

Sound travels fast in water, while banal intent
carries on wind. I span the difference,

distance between abating and loss, my arms
open as wide as a cross, the way I used

to mime, *I love you **this** much.* My fingertips,
twirl, dancers under masked moon,

stretch to reach back to the only heat
they find. Did you perceive

the shift? One of us became separate, the other
whole. Like when faith fails and the Bible

abstracts. Jesus becomes a kind, wronged mere
man. I suffer no crisis of conscience in the profane,

no loss of joy. Compassion ignites. Divine
space grows — light in the Potomac, Ursa Major,

Cuckold Creek, a wink from a stranger, the brushing
off of dirt. Your spirit, tangled in want, reaches through

the impossibility of phone lines. You speak
into my ear to craft intimacy of our past —

secluded beach where clothes peeled off, skins
of snakes on patrol at the shore. I don't respond

because I once loved you. Now I cradle extraction
of scent-memory from playing house. How you

withheld gleaming in my darkness but I still
shined. I hear your vacancy, but I am full.

Alive on Cuckold Creek I

My thalassophobic daughter monitors
my adventures. I'm known to cross unfamiliar
waters, over my head, with wind, stinging
invertebrates, and at times little steam.

We doubt she could save me from my own wild
or threats below. She resists walking
onto the dock, settles on the porch, immerses
herself in different dangers — TikToks on climate

change, being young and radically considerate.
We doubt I could save her either, my futile
suggestions for 20th century pastimes, my worry
and generosity. But like my mom says before I hit I-95

going 110 kilometers per hour for ten hours,
Call when you get home.
Her old jalopy shakes above 50 and seems
to have narcolepsy. No one points out the inanity

of the ask. We smile and hug and maybe
thoughts of her waiting prop my eyes open
against lullaby of tires in the drowsy last stretch
of Maryland. Maybe my girl looks up from

the news to watch me glide just before being crushed
by the story's punchline. The ways we save each other,
keep us afloat. As the sky blushes pink, I turn
home to her, despite temptation to head into night.

Thalassophobia is fear of deep water.

Alive on Cuckold Creek II

for Coley

In its grazing rock and marsh splendor
nothing invites abandon like water. I will

go in, be rocked, claim buoyancy. I promise
to be careful, as heartened by your concern

as I am the glinting creek. We watch the bloom
of jellyfish from the dock and I understand

to protect my skin. Drag a kayak through muck
until free to glide. Later you ask, *Didn't you*

take the dead crabs at the edge as a sign? or *how you*
fell in mud? Oddly, I did not. My mission
was clear — take to water.

The Great Blue Heron doesn't flinch as I approach.
He looks into the middle distance, watching
souls mingle with clouds. The reptile I mistake
for a crocodile slithers closer, a spirit guide

past piers and chairs until light peeking from
cabins are left with plastic and metal far behind.
It's just me, current, and other creatures inhaling
earthen musk in brackish water I scoop with palms,

to sprinkle on limbs and chest, a kind of baptism.

I turn at the dam, row faster toward your waiting. Plan
to step on the dock to subvert mud — Kablooey!

Don't remember the tipping or the boat-drag-swim
then creep through sludge. You tell me I cursed a lot.

Don't remember tentacles brushing my arms and legs
but I burn and itch. I remember you ask, *What can I do?*

You feed me Sun Chips and wine, poke fun. My fool-
hardiness and your care level our dynamic,

your growing up and my return to my pre-Mama offbeat
propel us toward hilarity, connection. You hope I learn

a lesson, but it would be a perfect dream to do again.
Nothing invites abandon like water. I go in.

Long Winter on the Northshore

Every secret makes a being where I
    was otherwise a ghost,
a walking stick, or excuse for another's
    short-temper. What lacks

is oxygen, burned by bitters, alcohol,
    rapid-breath of sobs and snores.
I stay awake, fold myself away,
    fuel nothing with little sips of air.

Tender skin surrounded
    by sharp nails, forked-tongues, cold.
I'll tear it off for moments
    of attention, a recess from lonesome.

I build a home in gaze on nests, naked
    branches, shadows on snow — I collect
into soft closets, flower pots, sugar bowls —
    transform loneliness to solitude.

There are always cats and trees.
So what I'm saying is that I'm lucky.

Celebration of Survival

Sometimes they converge to justify
every prior moment — Time,
temperature. Above frozen

lake in morning *see how it changes*
from solid to liquid, how sun spreads
itself across slick, kisses
your nose through wisps
of smoke, cigarette dangling
from your lips; how white caps

from last night rest like glass. I brought
only a small knapsack but now
see I overpacked.

See how my frozen
hand warms in yours, how clothes
peel off like days, while Aion erases
years and asks *what would you trade*
for youth? Nothing, we agree.

Aion - Greek God of cyclical time

Seems We Fall Into Buddhist Surrender

It's not like it breaks, or splits
    in two, this heart of mine.

        It peels.
Contrasts how yours burns. We suffer
      despite ourselves. We find

        our good time, bound
    to weights

of longing, little losses
        everytime you say

"later." Maybe if measured, we're more
rich than broke. Hard to say. I make

    a practice
        of appreciating things I can have

in lieu of your company — layers of warm
clothes, crunchy cold earth underfoot, shadows
    and the sound of the sea in irrationally
        brisk

wind. I weather myself, peel after
        frost. You char, become

    harder to burn —

    ways we make ourselves
happy even if altogether aside from love.

Glint of Gold

Blink as slow as you'd like, yawning window.
I'll just close your eyes. Do the insides of your

lids predict moon phases or is she stunted,
a crescent, a child's sketch? We all keep

a little yellow tucked out of view, in folds of
knuckles, hum to it at 2 a.m, credit the color

and song for getting us through; it sure as hell
isn't the quiet. Body-escaped fears

from forebearers and teachers walk around boneless,
hiss in wiring and window frames—

encourage hiding. Still, sometimes at night it rains.
We disrobe to dance; unfathomable to stay soggy

without the drying sun. And that's more of an answer
than shapes can offer — that there will be weather,

heels to kick up; that we see our fingers
even in darkness, and find sleep before dawn.

A Month of Thursdays

I miss you in the night we disappoint
each other — hold
the space in

solitude. Hiding
breaks us past repair.

Music is balm and tinder. You sing
loud, toggle between keys.
I hum as my life
depends on it. In stillness and sleep
wishes tarnish on our tongues.

It's no different from past Thursdays except

hope retreats. Still, I
stare-dream you blast not "In Your Eyes"
but "Maybe I'm Amazed" outside
my ground-level window.

I open
you step inside.

Fetch my gaze, shake thoughts like a *Magic 8* Ball,
"My reply is no."

How does mourning shape nights of conjuring
a spirit still
dancing within his bones?

Every day I'm relieved

you live and to not see you —
lengthening hair I no longer
cut, quick-witted fingers.

I take scissors to carve
photos along the curve of my waist, your
hip, where our bodies meet, place
you between pages in my nightstand drawer.

My dad passed on a Thursday.
It was already my Day of Failing.

The cardinal outside my
window whistles, *You read me all wrong.*

I tell him he's not off the hook.
None of us choose
what we symbolize.

Split myself in half to make my will
yield to absence. Today, I don't try
to make light of the day. I
pour propensity to love for love's sake
into the grass for the dead.

Most days are shrines where I grow
roses and cacti. Today needs
burlap, rain, a rock in a glass
of gin with bitters before

forgiveness of orgasms
and detachments.

Tonight's no different except

the flower moon glows
with such beauty as to crush me
even if full moons weren't
our space to rest in each other.

If Everything Changes, Why Not This?

My mistake — tattooing your name on my tongue.
I keep my mouth closed more often now. Shame
is the man who pays the devil on my shoulder.

Sometimes, I call him "friend."

Leverage consciousness with your consonants.
Nothing tastes right, until after sunrise,
foray into cold, sips of bitter coffee,

a new man — what hurts a bit, distracts. Hope
from this dementia-like
hangover shakes me back

and forth — settles into morning bloom. Until bitters, but…

That's not what I mean. It's that tattoos weigh
nothing and I need ballast. My head tilts, my back
curves, wants to paint the horizon. Hands

wrap presents, count bills, mix flour, unable to
hold on. Shame is a woman-mother who feeds
the devil lines of children's self-disdain.

I seek oracles, gems, God, spirits to grant me alchemy
to change their falsehoods to mirrors of the bright
casts they glow, as they are, to no avail.

It's a bit much and others suffer losses
if I erode.

Shore me up from my bend, tip, slip. Just one finger,
    one hour one day a week, to show
        care. I dreamed a wish, a mistake.

Sullied mornings contract, forget.
    I tattoo a lightbulb below my ear; pedal fast

to ignite it. Your legs are stronger, but I can't ask
    to borrow them because they're strangers: now,
        I shine light on the devil's lips.

*

Age Out of Influence

I'm done readying "out there" for you.
You prefer to stay in; don't much like
the elements, shirk from the sun that
glistens off your tears and still, that smile.

We teeter on the edge
like when you dangled off
the bed at three-years-old, the crook
of my arm suspending you in

mid-air, in my sleep. When you
leaned out the window of the train, I
held your shirttails. Scenes change fast.
My veneer burned off slow. Calm, festive,

mature — contrived no more. I
strip it off. Now just a woman with
fire and rolling eyes. You go to your church
and I'll go to mine. You're grown enough.

My time is no longer yours, unless
you want it. (I pray you want it.) But it's not for
the scores of well-intentioned others. Every one
of them can cook well, control their kids, keep

better house; hang wet topcoats on my shoulders.
They're not wrong. But like you at four, I now
prefer to be naked. Besides, I like best what I
can't control — cats, water-colors, storms, you.

Unironic Love Poem to my 17-Year-Old

for Quinn

The you in the magic
that dance-like twisted my
swollen postpartum body
to keep you sky face up
when the dog pulled us
tripping down over wires.

The you in superhero suits,
haunted houses in June, ironic
poems still true, nonsensical
essential laughs, courage in
a world of judge-ophiles, in-
your-own-timeness, in your

being proof of miracles.
I don't care if you're a boy
or girl or other, straight
or gay, if you listen or
ignore everything I say.
You choose any name, I'll

love them all. You fall
anywhere, on any spectrum —
left, further left, quirky, quiet,
perceptive, bright — the point
of my devotion. The you
is protected in the parts of me
I most revere.

Falling

When the world feels like a baby pulled
up over barbed wire
and like the barbed wire, or more
like the pulling, the tight

grasp, silence is in order.
No pause comes
in the yelling, in gravity. We all might

fall as stars, as rain, as empires do.
Iron for the fence demands
the red of rocks, gorgeous in soil, in cliffs,
generous, even informing

drill bits that sculpt or steal
from it. The collisions
grow creatures we see only for an instant
upon waking before they dissipate and we rise

to meet another clash or fall
again in love with a baby whose skin
is not torn.

Hearing Voices: State of Being

I burrow
in your voice, pull
gritty undulations above
my head and hide.

I seek your advice
but need your tones, all
gravel and boom, grounding
even when unclear or cruel.

Your laugh pops, a firecracker
off-season, startles and demands
less so now that you're gone, silent
embers adrift below caws of crows.

I Just Want to Cut Your Nails

Lost agility, through age and belief
    that your mind was above
banality of exercise, you
    can't reach your toes.

Was it disgust for appendages so far
    from your heart — so weird in
acceptance of dirt and weight and
    being cloistered? These

feet that ground and move you; invite
    you to dance; deserve care because
they too are you. So gently I'd position
    clippers while singing a tune to distract

you from sharp. There would be no awkward
    looks; my eyes focussed on the task to
trim, smooth, then sooth with drops of
    lemongrass oil. You would no longer

scratch your leg when roaming in sleep.
    Your-sized shoes will fit.
You reject off-hand, as though it's an offer and not
    a request. As though it's for you and not for me.

As We Rely on Each Other

Take the sky from me for a moment,
unwrap my arms from the clouds.

Make it weigh less — this aging, this hydrologic cycle,
this gravity, being left, remaining.

Squeeze sugar water rain into earth for our dead;
into my hair, clothes, make me less buoyant. Still I float.

A shimmer of hummingbirds drinks with our departed.
That and wind, never extracted from weather; arms

never extracted from holding; and a short rest are enough.
I spread my wings, gather back the blue yonder you took

from me. Make a home of falling,
carrying, knowing nothing will drop.

A Good Life in Which Quinn Lives

Any moment, you could be
wind, sand, stardust. I
am unsure whether to say

"can't" or "don't want"
this world without you.
At this now, we all

have skin and weather.
That you've almost
died keeps me humble,

glad for rain, teetering
on the grateful side
of mourning.

If Words, Like Love, Like Poems, Never End

for Clifford Bernier

Before opening, I light candles, incense
*flames rising like the chants of monks.**
I bake fish, for scent of sea more than my
off and on *pescado* ways. The wind

is cold today. I sojourn to forest and beach,
imbibe on your verandah. Harmonica phrases
quiver through the doorway. Sun glare, wist,
pollen seeping through old window frames, and

God knows what brings the migraine that has your
lines waving and dancing. Already adrift, I welcome

microgravity, transience, floating, the spark
of light in which we may not even be finite.

*from *Kathmandu*,
Earth Suite (p. 10).

Soft Side of Gold

When hands clasp, glimmer's felt
in blood, carried
in a wave or forest bathing.
Changes everything.

Fireflies ignite the swish
of my hair, always popping
from another direction while I
feed log after log to this insatiable

fire that won't go out, despite
the heat. It dares
me to expose; find love in softness
of thighs rubbing together.

Rain represses nothing, but offers
percussion to my (I now
realize) beautiful hum.

I carry a house with windows that won't close,
grateful for the dysfunction.
I run to the west side in the evening and drink
sunset, elongate it in a squint, carry gold into night.

*

Gust

C'mon concrete, dissolve. I jones
to kick-up dust. Artifice crashes fuming
waves; down they fall — I just want
the salt. Inhalation of sunrise traded
for rock-heavy greetings in sexless mornings.

I now idle in bird-song, open
windows, irrelevant walls. Flight
stays well after the going.

You were loud wind between tall buildings.

If I pay closer attention before moonrise,
will you stay? Don't churn
blustery distraction into meaning — poor
excuse for chemistry.

Some dance on the head of jewel bearings; they
must keep the spinning earth
in balance. If a wave crashes
too close, one might slip in time. lose
direction. Eaten by the sea
bodies shed noise, take off as music.

Celebration of Divorce

If then what started ablaze in hunt

for constellations and curb-hitting

distraction, dimmed to warm glow

of "Once I was loved by a man who

gave me everything," and I learned

to keep it safe, there's no room

to squeeze in regret. Free space

gorgeous as his mouth was; as is

each going our own way—

Oh, I'm a pinball delighted

with ricochet and bells! The only thing

I can predict is my rolling on more

shiny, smooth for having been a wife.

To Dally in Fibonacci Spirals

Join me to whisk away from judgment and
chores — fugitives from space and time.
Don't you know we can
open them both? like sweet

pineapples, malleable cauliflower. We too
make delicious treats from being

hearty and rough. Mind your tender
shoulder, but still throw
worry to the stars and sling

that guitar onto your back. Let's flee from lines to
dance in spirals, pass our past, run to the old
swing set by the abandoned barn to fly

above the hurricane. Come to me in your

empty hours. We'll bring restlessness to a boil until
it evaporates off to sleep.

Slip ourselves into space between like
chicory petals, pinecone scales, waves.

My Plan to Play Guitar Well Before I Die

Intros speak in wind
and waters, *Soar*
or swim before the flood.

Sometimes I sink, savor
even gravity.

I dizzy from somersaults these
days but still dive between
crescendos and caesuras.

I consume movement, dare
bold aspirations to create — set

fire to silence.

Wish to song-pierce the skyline in staccato
Oriole-like bursts. I see the madness.
Still, I want.

Guitar strings roughhouse with beachgrass, clap
to Wind's baton, the only
place time makes sense.

I drink elixirs of jade and mercury to add years
of possibility.

Measuring Your Death as More than My Fair Share of Time

Written and abandoned script crawls
into rain and cellophane wrappers to tap
on windows in want to reunite

with your fingers and throat.
These almost-were words compete
with your quiet, or silence.

Did you say anything at all?
Your eyes speak like a girl trapped
in a bottle, one that may run ashore,

or a genie who'll let loose, float
in the *Ow* after your last sharp inhale.
No light makes sense against

your closed eyes. Not the parking lot
fluorescent din, not the glowing phone
through which my lover mocks me because

I lost my car. How might I find
anything in the day I lost you? Cars jump
away when we blink, shrapnel
in the dump where I collect crickets.

Creases of the Year

Clouds hunger, beg the sun to melt off
the lakes. Sip the vapors.

Sometimes we all like to rain.

After birthday parties
and fireworks, below resolutions dimmed
to a single
burning ember, no holiday lit
backdrop to photo ops, Time
threatens *I'll wait.*

We stand in bread lines scratching
our heads against day-to-day
wars; wonder how light
can be held formless in cupped hands. Sway
to the tune of grumbling stomachs.

Forget to recall who we aim
to be; that we make history
with every smile, the phantom
of our best self.

To resurrect aspirations — Ghost Dances; only require
music; nothing more
than instrument, or voice, fingertips,
memory of a tune that starts
a spark, fire
always in our grasp.

Wealth of Collaboration

Only a little help to tap out a rhythm,
maybe drum, that's all I ask
And don't accuse me of poverty –
I'm strapped with guitar and pluck my adornments.

Maybe drum, that's all I ask,
share a beat to quicken my heart.
I'm strapped with guitar and pluck my adornments.
I don't want your diamonds.

Share a beat to quicken my heart
and don't accuse me of poverty.
I don't want your diamonds,
only a little help to tap out a rhythm.

Dynamics

Instruct the kids to keep voices
"on zero." I hoped instead to whisper
"pianissimo." Another little lost
enchantment and a pixie
falls dead.

Add pressure to crescendo.
Still, remember fragility
of folds, hairs, strings, gears.

Everything strained may
break — voice, heart, and peering
into clouded memories included.

Does the peering break
or do the eyes themselves? You tell me. I already
fucking forget. But I know
scales, resonance, elasticity.

Rubber bands speak endurance, then
a little tragedy when brittle and snap.

They never care, calling out, "Project!"
like we're an opera, 'though they don't know Italian.
American suburbs hold
power in soft, humming, whistles. I hear
trains far off.

Wind Also Wants to Move

You collect patience in pauses to wade
through my weeping, tedious as
as the katydids' unbroken static I miss
come November. I hang up.

A train whistle whispers from
four miles off, *you can still*
move through space. I study
the tune of wheelsets on
steel, hold my breath.

Early cardinals bring you
back, the boys with bright
red like your door and our
hearts, beating less-than-true;
not sold yet verges on not ever.

Do you feel it grow in your
not-hollow bones? How we're closer
to death than youth? But still could be
beautiful as jays. I pretend

crows bring good luck — common, plentiful
generous with chatter, their cardinal-less-ness
some relief. One screams

from my bough. Makes me look
up, expansive as sky, as death.

A Month of Thursdays: Epilogue

Each moment extends a blanket, mirror,
hammer, wine, pen — chance
to choose what to hold. Have we

learned differences between
perspective and bald-faced lies yet?

Back to the start. Truth won't be out of grasp,
despite our feathers. We won't both clip
wings and refuse to stand,
not even in the eye of the moment
we'll need to trick ourselves out of regretting.

Today's no different from past Thursdays except

songs burnt and bitter after
the incineration now remind me less
of him. I need only maple leaves
and honey of my blood to brighten them.

I now sing
for no man.

We mask (no more) too quiet
for being forced to mask weirdness.

How do we line up according to height, or first
initial, go through the turnstile, to claim
an order that will kill many of us?

I'm sorry but... Is wholly different
from I'm sorry.
I respect you, but... Is wholly different
from I respect you.

Sweat and shiver in equal measure
to sunbaths, moondances. Embrace
hurt without connected
guise of sincerity.

Pre-forgetting becomes learning, like all history, all
becoming. I was born on Thursday, a day of thunder

under clouds that dropped nothing.
This morning the crow cawed, *Let it.*

I thank him for being brazen, wise,
even with forced humility
from what we choose him to symbolize.

As I seal myself with wax, also trying to mend
a loose fabric of *we the people*, I search in
heterogeneous as unity. I
hum tunes of love for love's sake
into wind to shore up the fragile of us.

Sometimes we don't recover, instead grow
gills, bend spines. This day needs loti,
mariposa lilies, as well as roses and a glass
of rainwater for each 8 billion of us before

forgiveness of procreation,
attachments and walls.

Tonight's no different except

thunder moon illuminates
rise of fewer easy breaths,
falls in truth, and the beauty
of lament in her glow.

*

In the Morning, I Linger in Thoughts of You

I rise late, your antics stuff every color
you lent my world into a knapsack.

You peel your stained glass heart
from my window like an ocean-wet

handkerchief. I smell salt and seaspray.
I wear rosary beads down to grains

of sand, rub worry dolls until unraveled
threads bejewel my hair. If *Love*

is an active noun like *struggle, missing*
is like *escape*. I feel my heart pound

calling beyond function. I pay
phantom pain no mind. See the true

miracle —that mourning does end.

Near to Life

for Venus

We walk slow on your bum knee
take breaks to tease out your girl
crazy, my boy crazy, weight
of absence that tasks
our joints and always
the artists with bum hearts.

We speak of our energetic
sons, the way they settle in
for snuggles when sick. Our
frenzy for their good health.

We swim in blue sky, against
currents of air, clouds in shades
of dusk, of bruises; wind strongest

against your breast. Vigor
and power reduces from
what you had grown —
tsunamis, thunder, green vines
through clay, one blossom.

I feed you ice chips. You smile
over chapped lips that catch
on dry teeth. Desert
under fluorescent lights.

I don’t want a day to dawn
without you, so I stay
awake. Skin and limps,
dimples and crushes, all
must be laid down.

Sanctuary!

If I must be in solitary, make it space
with extra rooms where I can gather speed,

if not from me from the fear I held
a moment ago. Let me fire my blood

in yellow halo-light outside my skin, hollow
my bones, call *Sanctuary!* from acquaintances

and news. I'll hum my breath out to grant it
some absolution in song; fashion wings

to know pedestrians from a distance. After all
what good are hands when we can't touch.

Tilting in Diffused Night-Light

It starts as a gathering
like the wind-swept dunes we used
for King of the Mountain or like clusters

of spring leaves coaxed
from bark. So really it starts with the tilt
of the earth, that leans me

off-kilter, balance-dancing, toward you. —
There's no explaining the popping bright
of fireflies, or sheen and float

of bubbles forged with mere breath, or
how the full moon dares us
when hidden from view.

There's no predicting when wits will fail
to gather about me, but it starts
when our tongue tips touch.

Bucket List Accomplished

No word as pretty as aurora borealis, a whisper
to evoke love, so far away. Under light, hold

night in palm, tilt and pivot labradorite, watch
rays and swirls of greens, blues, yellows iridescent.

Stop at bend closest to rapids on the towpath, feel
the spray from Niagara Falls flutter on closed

eyelids; the rush in your ears. Paint your door cerulean.
Open Greece every time you come home. Pretend

your deaf and illiterate when your landlord protests. Eat
olives and hummus saturated with oil, lemon and sea.

Lean full-front into an Oak and look up at branches that
reach impossibly high. Caress bark and bid sequoias well.

Paint the door back to white. Imagine a wedding, a Darlin'
waiting at home. Enter Wonderland in study of reflection

of switchgrass that circles the creek, not on, now in, the water.
Of things cheap may seem — poor, want to squirrel away

for kids, cha-cha'ing with rainy day fund — none
equate to lack. To slip off grandiose — another means

to fortune. A bonfire on the beach under stars? Rather, pour
something spiced in a glass, sit with candle flame and croon.

St. Cecilia

Three days with head not quite severed,
neck more robust than a log.
Fibers held fast, separated
slow; time to put affairs in order.

Saints and their gruesome deaths
for the love of God. Those in hell
on earth and their gruesome deaths
not so different, the violence.

Some venerated for chastity,
some for precisely the passions
Saints denied. In the end, it's all
extremes of love; what cuts

life short, inspires posthumous praise.
While the rest lay waiting, waiting
this long life, not able to put order
to anything; never knowing

when it'll end, with just enough grace
jingling like pocket change to get by.

Suicide Road

It's around the bend
under the skyway, the dark
stretch, the jumping
leg of road where echoes
of bumps and thuds
dance with stereo's bass,
where false shadows paint
dents on car hoods.

"Ideation" is a dumb
way of saying idea. Thought
is already action. Just ask
an artist, inventor,
one who lives long enough
to put things in the world.

Crosses ornament
the shoulder like
rosary beads,
birds on a wire,
wildflowers. Maybe
collateral damage
of shouldering
too much or not finding
other humans that gift
pride in this species.

I white-knuckle
too slow, dangerous

as others whiz past.
Jerk the wheel as
imagined bodies
plentiful as ghosts
fly past.

Let Them Fortify and Buzz

Two mosquitoes fly
into my open window.
I let them buzz weightless
in streamlined splendor.

Let them land, on my
thigh, a lily pad, fingers
flowers, nectar my
blood. Not because I
love mosquitoes

nor that I've never killed.
I just can't stand another
leaving me weaker than
when they arrived.

Twenty Years is Too Much a Part of Me to Ever Be Past

for Coley

Clouds drift east toward
the city, the Bay, the ocean.
She'll rest here beneath them, just shy
of the water, while I move west,
between city and mountains, to where
there's less, not even her now.

I see how false idols grow power, as I
pray to every statue, every brick and stone,
to protect her. What else can I do?

I thought I built a nest for her to fly
from, return to. But realize now, I
nested in her; left my absurd
youth in the plastic hospital bassinet
and took shelter in her need and
open heart, vast space of
imagination. I could never
want to die as long as she's alive.

Before morning light, I kneel and
pray, thankful and beseeching. By now
By now I know life can be more
gorgeous than my asks, so I keep

them vague and metaphoric — to contain
ill-suited tears, to soar, celebrate

her growing up. It doesn’t matter
the direction I look now, gaze softened.

About the Weather

In windless sky, beneath solitary cloud anchored
to granite, he says,
"I Am Terrible with Weather."

Fire can't spread, nor rain fall, so earth sleeps,
not bereft. He jostles her awake, laughs

louder than polite. Pins hope on that one cloud,
"It's a brand new toy," he says. *I see a wheel.*

We agree it's the same and when at last it turns
everything changes. He says,

"I Am Terrible with Weather,"
camouflaged in 21st century-comfort, ceiling and roof,

a cold-blooded human who prefers it brisk.
He paints atmosphere, light — gravity eats it all.

What he means by,
"I Am Terrible with Weather,"
is *forecasts be damned.* In scorched overhead light,

predictions wrap plans around crumpled paper,
tin foil, storybook images, doomsday clutter;

never capture snowflakes, moonbeams,
a drop on exposed skin.

*

Maybe Keep What Makes Us Mad

While all eyes are on the sunrise, a shade
of yearning we'll try to recreate later on lips,

you steal a slice of moon. Full, it made mischief
with want, sleep, waves — things that might kill

more surely and kindly than tedium. Sun holds
us in her glare while ground is washed away. You pierce

the gray aglow sliver we now call yours into blue
like an ice axe. None of us fall. And the moon, now

diminished, calms. So in a way, you save us all.
Although legend has it, there are more ways to survive

than there are to die. Don't talk to me about the speed
of the spinning earth. I may get sick. Just keep the fragment

tucked in your breast pocket. Take it out when light's in short
supply to give you a small measure of comfort. Or if willing

to brave the cold again, reunite it, if whenever we get better
at body surfing, reckless enough to love the full moon.

The Sound of Absence

Before the flame, I see only fire, hear
only crackles that pop off straight away.

Inhales dry my throat sore —
picture wind as waves, far away.
                    Forget breath.

Watch shapes dance light's musings
from one candle behind closed eyes.

How did I get here? to doing nothing
in this day full of possibility?

I take to the floor to forsake doing for the sake
of wanting to be free of want — to get to the end

of this to-do list long as my cat's tail that bops
my cheek from my lap; to be full and fit

and drunk; running outside and asleep. This want
for my phone to ring, your voice in my ear.

I quiet to hear the drum in the divide

Evidence of Life Being Better

I settle into daily devotional dialogues
with my child this season like it's my job
and church. How to let him know life gets
better in these sharp days from his vantage

of years stretching from brutal youth?
My evidence is intangible, despite the space
I create for him to unfurl the stuff of mamas'
nightmares. And I'm all here for it, grateful

his voice carries us into the future. Where
might a mom collect such patience
if not from life's charm? — birds' jazzy reveille,
spread of mauve light, wind-blown-leaves,

my personal Innisfree, the shoring up
by one friend, maybe two, who, solid, just stays.

When December Becomes Home

In the morning of three fires, trees
hold their breath while I sneeze
                  on truth absent words.

Even music holds its tongue.

Flame, Tell me about belief. All the light
I need through night and night
                  and day, holding hook
of lamp, no place to secure.

I awaited Winter's bare branches to see
where bird nests hide. Limbs forgive
gravity, extend sky space sans flight.

Tomorrow we meet beneath
naked branches; match skin to voice,
to notes; plant calls of crows, of hawks,
of sparrows, on the long staffs of our sleeves;

touch fingertips with the gravitas
of a 16 year old's mixtape.

D.

Take my veins and make
a bungee cord to jump
off and away while my
blood circles the microgravity
of my body knowing
no aqueducts, no confines. Take
this salt, wine, and soup too.
We survived on them long enough.

The night you got cross
that I missed reading
your mind visits. Enough. I feel
guilty though you were probably
drunk. Were we ever sober?

Regions away I hunt
to alter consciousness — sleep deprivation,
dreams, ceremonial rites,
meditation. Lucky to ever
assign a single letter in script
to a friend, two, "Hell is murky.
Fie, my lord, fie." Some Loves
grow too pervasive to reign
into a name. But all turn away
in time. Name, initial, name,
quiet.

I find a bowl the shade
of plates you bought and fill
it with honey; with grits

and butter but mostly honey.
I feed it to the dog to help
him take meds. You'll miss
his death I suppose; our
mourning, my rebirth.

I hung the world on your sigh for too long.
Take my letters and make
a paper-rope. Tie it to your waste,
a pulling chord,
someone else collect you to
a platform high above
mountains. Do you see
in the clouds? Shapes of an old
cocker spaniel, old women, your initial?
Do you see how the wind
transforms them to birds and ships?

Empathy

Do not go into the mire as though you might offer coattails to kite
escape to fresh space. It's too hot for jackets and besides, we set

them aside long ago. We travel only with skin that fails to hold
in heat from combustion hearts. There's no denying attraction to warmth,

sound, dying to save another. The wail of a witch at the stake resonates
the same as a banshee's warning; both beguile, but only one might

be saved. Loud-eyed do-gooders rebranded Sympathy as pity,
although she's the best understanding we had before throwing

ourselves into the fire. All the green tea and dark leafy vegetables
in the world won't protect us from our own good intentions.

Creative Seeing

for Grace Cavalieri

I know the pull to reach into depths
of dark and heavens. I will grasp

soft, pointed truth of a moment,
a movement. Called by her illumination

of space, color. Her name — a smile,
that guides and propels us toward

the action of words. Such a slight woman
to reach her arms around the whole world —

around laureates, the obscure, every bombshell
and mother. Perhaps she descends

from Aliens to whom some credit
ancient wonders, or she is the wonder, making

Poets feel like miracles walking in a world
of miracles; rendering forms supernatural.

If I'm merely a player, may she be the playwright. Even as
supporting character or as a bad guy, I know I'll glimmer.

Memory's Intrusion

Imperceptibly small, this shard of glass that takes
shelter in my fingertip, begs
to be scratched, soaked; to take

the throne in this velvet day. It robs
charm from squirrels who tangle in whirl
of black and gray yin and yang; I barely
notice. I miss delight in birdsongs,

sunlit moss, cats. Remembering you here
is like that — a thief, a tether,
a broken music box that double dog dares

my chaotic heart to pit-a-pat faster. I look
to the glove you threw down
for a moment. That's all it takes
to miss the take-off of the sparrow.

Stars Bend Light, Erase Habit of Devotion

An injurious name persists
calling out from innocent places.
Whispered too long it turns stranglehold
to the future, forked in rocks and wings.

Deceit is impalpable, not
impossible. It grows like weeds in collusion
with desire and hope. A place of light may save
from harm, if it embodies enough facets.

Oh Stars, be my falling and catch me.
Ante up erasures (unname, reframe), stash
memory away, until weak, collapsed, exploded
or cooled in any of your spaces.

-tuck behind backlit clouds
-throw into Betelgeuse to burn
-sink beneath swimming sparkles in dome-skied Tennessee
-cover in oil swirls of dots and pentagons that fuel wind and long-necks
-bury past upward gaze from car hood in boosy Florida cemetery
-drown below your reflection in the river
-fold into the silver side of a two-toned sequin shirt

A lie no longer the shortest distance between
two points; assent no longer my lingering folly.
We rewrite futures, the Stars and I, rehab
thoughts. Even after rainy nights, I awake to starlight.

What people are saying...

If we could take some syllables out of *Love Letters from Cuckold Creek* to inject into the algorithms now making A I, we would make its future language crystalline and kind. It would provide the necessary gene now missing from robotics—a feminine intelligence, with a mother's nurturing love; and the tenacity of a performer: ("…I now sing for myself…") Kristin Kowalski Ferragut is also a musician, you can tell by her cadence, the lifted phrase, the lilt, and the esthetics using word and space skillfully placed. Just hear lines like: "I don't want a day to dawn/ without you, so I stay/ awake." This book is way overdue. I would have always wanted it.

Grace Cavalieri
Maryland's tenth Poet Laureate

The world needs a place like Cuckold Creek where one can immerse in Kristin Kowalski Ferragut's poetry, keep it in our mind's eye and remember it as we catch sight of a cloud "Take the sky from me for a moment, unwrap my arms from the clouds/As We Rely on Each Other" and smile thinking of her venture into the wetlands under the watch of her grown child "…in brackish water I scoop with palms, to sprinkle on the limbs and chest, a kind of baptism/Alive on Cuckold Creek II" and recall the odes she wrote to her children. Loss, love, mourning, and nature are themes Kristin addresses and forges into one's mind. The world needs a copy of Cuckold Creek in their back pockets to give one "Sanctuary" with and through Kristin's poetic language "Even after rainy nights, I awake to starlight/Stars Bend Light, Erase Habit of Devotion."

kelly catharine bradley, author of *a gift* and *love, loss and the enormity of it all*

Reading Kristin Kowalski Ferragut's latest collection, *Love Letters from Cuckold Creek,* is like savoring a long, unrushed conversation with a friend. Each poem is intimate and personal, and yet, they are universal in their explorations of our emotional lives and loves. A biosphere of bruises and beauty. The richness of her language and freshness of her metaphors draw us even further into her world. From the "shimmer of hummingbirds" to a "stained-glass heart," she explores what it is to be human. At the heart of her work, we come to realize that her world is truly ours, too.

Le Hinton, author of *Elegies for an Empire*, *Sing Silence*, and *The God of Our Dreams*

Kristin Kowalski Ferragut is a poet-mom who lives in Maryland where she teaches, plays guitar, sings, rides her bike, and hosts readings and open mics. She is author of the full-length poetry collection *Escape Velocity* (Kelsay Books, 2021) and the children's book *Becoming the Enchantress* (Loving Healing Press, 2021). Her poetry has appeared in Beltway Quarterly, Anti-Heroin Chic, Fledgling Rag, Little Patuxent Review, and Gargoyle Magazine among others. In addition to poetry, she writes songs, short stories, and essays that can be found on her blog at https://www.kristinskiferragut.com/

www.ingramcontent.com/pod-product-compliance
Ingram Content Group UK Ltd.
Pitfield, Milton Keynes, MK11 3LW, UK
UKHW041316190726
13845UKWH00025B/303

9 789363 548190